Colorful Peacocks

by Deborah Underwood

PULL AHEAD BOOKS

Animals

Lerner Publications Company • Minneapolis

For John

Lerner Publications Company
A division of Lerner Publishing Group
241 First Avenue North
Minneapolis, MN 55401 U.S.A.

Website address: www.lernerbooks.com

Words in *italic* type are explained in a glossary on page 30.

Library of Congress Cataloging-in-Publication Data

Underwood, Deborah.
    Peacocks / by Deborah Underwood.
      p.   cm. — (Pull ahead books)
    ISBN-13: 978–0–8225–5930–6 (lib. bdg. : alk. paper)
    ISBN-10: 0–8225–5930–7 (lib. bdg. : alk. paper)
    1. Peafowl—Juvenile literature. I. Title. II. Series.
  QL696.G27U53 2007
  598.6'17—dc22   2005017977

Manufactured in the United States of America
1 2 3 4 5 6 — JR — 12 11 10 09 08 07

Look at this bird's beautiful feathers!

What kind of bird is it?

This bird is a peacock. Long *train feathers* trail behind a peacock.

Look at the spot at the end of a train feather. The spot is called an *eyespot*.

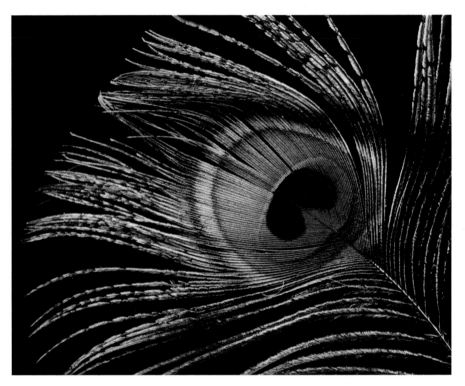

Can you see why?

Whoosh! This peacock lifts his train
feathers to make a beautiful fan.

Look behind this peacock's fan.

Can you see the peacock's short tail feathers?

All peacocks
are male.

They have bright blue
heads and necks.

Females are called *peahens*.

Peahens are not as colorful
as peacocks.

But peahens can fly better than peacocks. They do not have long train feathers to slow them down.

Together, peacocks and peahens are called *peafowl*.

Each peafowl has a *crest* on its head. A crest is a crown of feathers.

Peafowl live
in parks
and
gardens.

Peafowl can live
where it is very hot.

They can also live where it is
very cold.

During the day, peafowl stay on the ground.

At night, they *roost* in trees. They rest on the branches of trees.

A peacock's feathers blend in with the trees.

This helps a peacock hide from enemies.

Can you
find a
peacock in
this tree?

Peafowl eat insects, grains, fruits, seeds, and flowers.

Sometimes they eat frogs or snakes.
They drink from ponds or streams.

This peahen is about to lay eggs.
This piece of ground is her nest.

A peahen usually lays five
to eight eggs.

She sits on the eggs to keep
them warm.

Four weeks after the eggs are laid,
the baby birds *hatch*.

Baby peafowl are called *peachicks*.
The peachicks have fuzzy feathers.

Peachicks can stand soon after they hatch.

Their mother helps them find food.

Peachicks stay near their mother.
The peachicks can't fly. At night, they
stay on the ground with their mother.

Male peachicks don't have train feathers. Those feathers grow when a peacock is three years old.

Then the peacock can make a
feather fan. Whoosh! He is all
grown up.

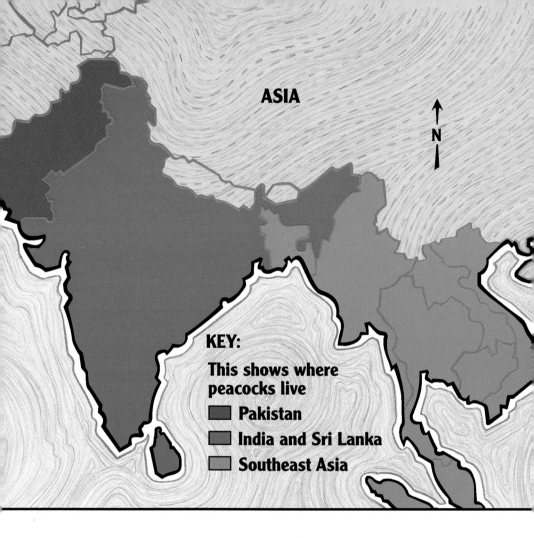

ASIA

N

KEY:

This shows where peacocks live

■ Pakistan

■ India and Sri Lanka

■ Southeast Asia

This is a map of Asia.
Where do peacocks live?

Parts of a Peacock's Body

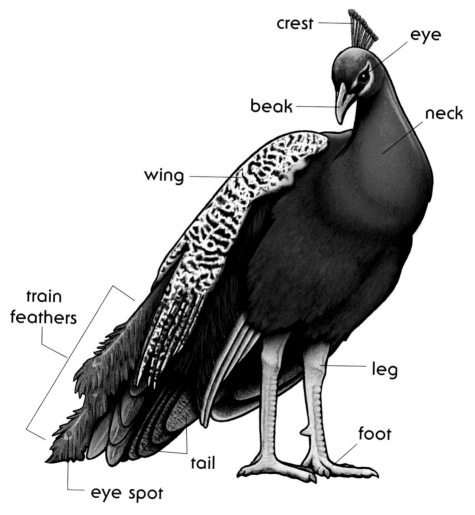

crest

eye

beak

neck

wing

train feathers

leg

foot

tail

eye spot

Glossary

crest: a crown of feathers on a peafowl's head

eyespot: a spot at the end of a peacock's train feathers

hatch: to come out of the egg

peachicks: baby peacocks and peahens

peafowl: the name for peacocks, peahens, and peachicks as a group

peahens: female peafowl

roost: to rest or sleep in the branches of a tree

train feathers: the long feathers that make a peacock's fan

Further Reading and Websites

Donaldson, Madeline. *Asia*. Minneapolis: Lerner Publications Company, 2005.

Animal Facts
http://wildwnc.org/af/peafowl.html

Enchanted Learning: All about Birds
http://www.enchantedlearning.com/subject/birds

Index

eating, 18–19, 24

eggs, 20–21

fan, 6–7, 27

feathers, 3–7, 10, 11, 16, 22, 26–27

flying, 10

roosting, 15

standing, 23

Photo Acknowledgments

The photographs in this book are reproduced with the permission of: © Dr. John D. Cunningham/Visuals Unlimited, front cover; © James P. Rowan, pp. 3, 10; © Allan Friedlander/SuperStock, pp. 4, 31; PhotoDisc Royalty Free by Getty Images, pp. 5, 27; © Glenn Oliver/Visuals Unlimited, p. 6; © Adam Jones/Visuals Unlimited, pp. 7, 8; © Carol Cook, www.peacockemporium.net, pp. 9, 18, 21, 22; © Michael H. Francis, pp. 11, 13; © Charles Fredeen, p. 12; © William Weber/Visuals Unlimited, p. 14; © Art Wolfe, p. 15; © Jerry Amster/SuperStock, p. 16; © Krupakar Senani/Oxford Scientific Films, p. 17; © Gerald Cubitt, p. 19; © Hopkins' Alternative Livestock, pp. 20, 26; © Mary C. Kauffman, pp. 23, 24; © Dr. Carleton Ray/Photo Researchers, Inc., p. 25.